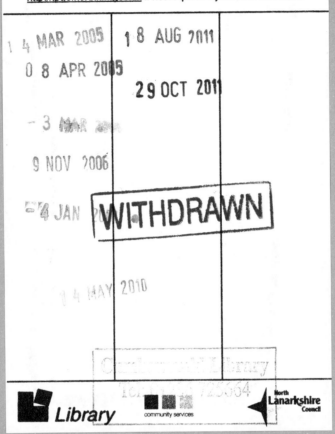

COPING WITH FRIENDS

BY KATE TYM AND PENNY WORMS

Raintree

www.raintreepublishers.co.uk
Visit our website to find out more information about **Raintree** books.

To order:
☎ Phone 44 (0) 1865 888113
🖹 Send a fax to 44 (0) 1865 314091
💻 Visit the Raintree bookshop at **www.raintreepublishers.co.uk** to browse our catalogue and order online.

First published in Great Britain by Raintree, Halley Court, Jordan Hill, Oxford OX2 8EJ, part of Harcourt Education.
Raintree is a registered trademark of Harcourt Education Ltd.

Raintree Editor: Kate Buckingham
Written by Kate Tym and Penny Worms
Packaged by ticktock Media Ltd.

With thanks to our expert advisers for their contributions and all the young people who gave us their stories.

Printed and bound in China by South China Printing Company.

ISBN 1 844 43410 9
08 07 06 05 04
10 9 8 7 6 5 4 3 2 1

British Library Cataloguing in Publication Data
Tym, Kate and Worms, Penny
Coping with Friends
302.3'4
A full catalogue record for this book is available from the British Library.

Acknowledgements
The publishers would like to thank the following for permission to reproduce photographs: Alamy: OFC, pp. **8** top, **19** top left, **19** top right, **20** top, **21** top, **24-25** centre, **26** top, **28** top, **30** top left, **30-31** centre, **32** top, **36** top left. Comstock: pp. **17** right, **33** centre. Creatas: p. **37**. Digital Vision: OBC, pp. **6** left, **9** top, **11** bottom, **18-19** centre, **25** top right, **38-39** centre. Roddy Payne Photographic Studio: pp. **4** top, **5** bottom right, **7** top right, **10** top, **12** top left, **13** top right, **14** top right, **15** top right, **16** centre, **22** top, **23** bottom, **27** top right, **34** top left, **34-35** centre, **35** right, **39** bottom right, **40** top left, **41** top right, **42** top right, **43** bottom right. Stockbyte: pp. **4-5** centre, **6-7** centre, **12-13** centre, **26** top, **29** right, **31** top right.

Every effort has been made to contact copyright holders of any material reproduced in this book. Any omissions will be rectified in subsequent printings if notice is given to the publishers.

All Internet addresses (URLs) given in this book were valid at the time of going to press. However, due to the dynamic nature of the Internet, some addresses may have changed, or sites may have changed or ceased to exist since publication. While the author and publishers regret any inconvenience this may cause readers, no responsibility for any such changes can be accepted by either the author or the publishers.

• CONTENTS • CONTENTS • CONTENTS •

INTRODUCTION

THE ART OF GOOD FRIENDSHIPS

FRIEND: Someone known well by another and regarded with liking, affection and loyalty.

Friends help you through the bad times, and are there to share the good times. They can give you advice on things that you might not want to share with your parents, they come in all shapes and sizes and can fulfil different roles in your life.

Some friends are simply mates – fun to socialize with or share a hobby or sport with. Some friendships go way deeper – they know your dreams and innermost secrets. Both types of friend enrich your life. The one thing all good friendships have in common is that they are based on trust. It's easy to make general chitchat with people but when it comes to really opening up and admitting your worries and fears, you only want to do that with someone you really trust.

'Friends are important.'

If you feel supported by a friend and are brave enough to open up, it can make your friendship all the more rewarding. Treat your friends in the way you would like to be treated yourself, and you should always have mutually fulfilling friendships. No friendship sails along without occasionally running into trouble. It could be a minor argument that lasts minutes or a major life-change that lasts years, but whatever it is, if you both value the friendship you'll make the effort to overcome whatever obstacles you might find in your way. And this book can help. It takes a close look at different aspects of friendship – how to make friends and how to fix a bust-up, what to do if you feel jealous or left out, and when it's time to end a friendship. It focuses on all manner of friendships from best friends to being friends with someone of the opposite sex. And when something comes between you, such as another person or your parents, this book shows you ways to deal with it.

'Real friendship is about trust.'

With true-life experiences and top tips to help you cope, it's not only full of useful information, but it may help you realize that, whatever the issue, you're probably not alone and … there's always a way to sort it out.

OUR EXPERT PANEL
THE EXPERTS GIVING ADVICE ARE...

Anita Jardine
Parent of two teenagers and experienced family practitioner. Currently employed as a school counsellor for the NSPCC and involved in providing a solution-focused service for young people and their parents/carers.

Simon Howell
Simon Howell is a social worker and family therapist. He works for the NSPCC.

Mac Buckley
Mac Buckley is a family liaison officer. She has worked in residential homes, schools and family centres for children and young people.

CASE STUDIES
Within each chapter are case studies – true stories about real people who have had some kind of problem to overcome. Read their stories, check out the experts' advice and learn what actually happened in the end. All the names of the contributors have been changed to protect their identity and models have been used for the photographs.

MAKING FRIENDS

HOW HARD CAN IT BE?

Making and keeping friends can be as natural as breathing to some people.
To others it can be an uncomfortable or even painful process.

TOP TIPS FOR MAKING FRIENDS

- **Smile**
  It's infectious, people will respond by smiling back.

- **Make eye contact**
  Eyes smile too, you know!

- **Ask questions**
  Asking a question is a great way to start a conversation.

- **Pay a compliment**
  It makes a person feel good and should start a conversation.

- **Don't make assumptions**
  Don't judge people before you know them. It might be that the person you think is 'too cool' or 'too loud' might be 'just right'.

- **Be confident**
  Act confident even if you don't really feel it. You've got a lot to offer a potential friend.

- **Be yourself**
  Don't try to be someone you're not.

Whether you find it easy or hard to make friends, there are times in your life when you have to do it. The most significant of these is when you change schools or move house. Many people's first reaction to change is to worry about it. This is perfectly normal – worrying is the brain's way of trying to solve problems.

But as much as worrying can solve your problems it can also magnify them. Your approach to life has a lot to do with how you cope with change. If you feel negative, or **pessimistic**, you will worry that you will never be able to make friends, or at least no friends as great as you had at your old school. Apart from a healthy dose of **optimism**, the other ingredient you need to make friends is confidence. It's difficult to feel confident when you are surrounded by strangers in an unfamiliar surrounding, such as a new classroom.

'I met people because I was always lost and they would show me the way!'

But if you can muster up even a little bit of confidence to say hello to someone on their own, or even smile at them, they might be relieved that someone is being friendly to THEM. It's different when you're the only stranger in a room full of friends – like when you join a school mid-term or start at a new club. That is a tougher test because everybody knows each other and you may feel like you will never fit in.

'I made friends by making people laugh.'

Be friendly to everyone and grasp any opportunity offered to join in. The more you chat with people and the more people you get to know in life, the better your chance of finding those special individuals who will remain lifelong friends.

8 WAYS TO MEET NEW PEOPLE

1 SIT NEXT TO THEM
Both at school and socially – you will immediately, or eventually, strike up a conversation.

2 SAY HELLO TO THEM
You'll appear friendly from the outset.

3 GRASP ANY OPPORTUNITY YOU GET TO JOIN IN
Don't restrict yourself to making friends at school. Join a club or sign up for an event.

4 ORGANIZE AN EVENT
Invite the people you'd like to get to know.

5 CHECK OUT YOUR NEIGHBOURS
Get to know people of a similar age in your street or village.

6 STRIKE UP CONVERSATIONS WITH PEOPLE WHO SHARE A COMMON INTEREST WITH YOU
You know you've got one thing in common so maybe there's more.

7 BE A TEAM PLAYER
Be happy to be part of a group.

8 MAKE SOMEONE LAUGH
Laughter is the best ice-breaker there is.

MY NEW FRIEND PUTS PEOPLE OFF

When Owen, 12, starts his new school he strikes up a friendship with a boy who turns out to be a bit weird. The worst thing is that people think Owen must be weird too.

> 'I've stopped hanging out with him now, but mud sticks! Not only have I got no friends, but everyone thinks I must be a geek.'

On the first day of my new school I got paired up with a boy in French who was really friendly.

At first it was great having someone to hang around with, as I didn't know a soul. But after a while, I realized that he was actually a bit of an annoying freak. He was always going on and on about really boring stuff. He had weird little habits too, and I mean WEIRD! People avoided him and because I was with him, they were giving me a wide berth too. I've stopped hanging out with him now, but mud sticks! Not only have I got no friends but everyone thinks I must be a geek too. I wish I'd never been friendly to him. How do I show people I'm all right really?

ASK THE EXPERTS...

Simon the social worker says...
Remember when you were at primary school you had plenty of good friends who enjoyed your company once they got to know you. This should help you regain your confidence in making friends. Keep trying to join in with others who share your interests and resist the temptation to score points by being unpleasant to the other boy — he has feelings too!

Anita the counsellor says...
Starting a new school is stressful. Making new friends quickly can help you settle in. It's great if you find you have lots in common, but tricky if that turns out not to be the case. The problem is dumping people doesn't make you look friendly! Show everybody you have a heart by smiling, chatting and listening to people. That way you'll find out which people you like too.

Mac the family liaison officer says...
Not everyone can be as cool as they'd like to be.
This boy is probably making too much of an effort to impress you and others at school, and as a result, comes across as nerdy and desperate rather than trendy. Don't worry about what other people think of you for hanging out with that boy. Once they make the effort to get to know you, they'll realize you are your own person, and somebody well worth being friends with.

THEY ALL HAVE MATES EXCEPT ME

When Lou, now 13, started at her new school she was worried about making new friends.

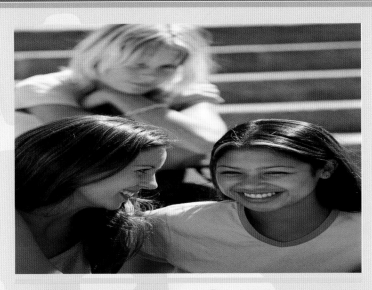

When I left primary school, I went to a different school to most of my mates.

I was worried about making new friends, because I'm quite shy. My mum was **sympathetic** but at the same time she just said, 'Well, there's nothing we can do about it. You'll just have to make new friends.' The first week was really awful. I was on my own most of the time and I felt on the verge of crying. The school seemed huge and everyone seemed to be laughing and joking. They all had mates already

'I'm quite shy and I was scared no one would like me.'

and I'm not confident enough to muscle in. The good thing, though, is that in classes you get put next to someone and it's easier to talk than not to say anything at all. At first it'd be just about the work. Then it was, 'What school did you go to before?' and 'Do you know so and so?' In my Geography lesson I sat next to a girl called Cara and she's really nice. I'd like to be friends with her but she has friends already. What can I do?

ASK THE EXPERTS...

Simon the social worker says...
It's really hard to be parted from a best friend and not surprising that you were sad for a while. Although it seemed as though everyone else was happy when you started the new school there were bound to have been others who felt just like you did. You've made a good start with Cara. Try making friends with the girls she already knows, as this can only help widen your social circle.

Anita the counsellor says...
Making friends can seem like a huge problem, something you'll never be able to do. This is weird because **friendship is natural.** We all need it and friendship possibilities are all around us like the air we breathe. The secret is to let friendship happen in its own time. And if you find yourself holding back or stopping people from getting to know you just relax and breathe!

Mac the family liaison officer says...
Being the new girl is never easy. You will feel as if everyone is looking at you, **but they won't be.** Don't stress out about things. Think how you can improve this friendship with Cara, and also chat with her friends — you may find you have even more in common with them than you do with her. Are there girls in any of your other classes that you might get on with, or who might know Cara and her friends? It's a good place to start.

CASE STUDY 3

I'M REALLY LONELY

Jess, 13, has lost her best friend and a group of girls are giving her a hard time.

'Things changed when my best friend started spending time with this other girl.'

When I started my new school, I was really excited. I knew lots of people from my primary school, so I wasn't worried about having to make new friends.

Things changed when my best friend started spending time with this other girl in our class. I was left on my own and I couldn't seem to make any other good friends. I was always on the outside of a group. Then this load of girls started giving me a hard time about being clever. One of them sat behind me in maths and seemed to have a real problem with me. Her group of mates started making my life hell – just snide comments, giggling and pointing, stupid stuff but it really got to me. So I ended up going to the library at breaks – I knew I wouldn't come across them in there! I now feel so out of it. I don't bother trying to make friends anymore. I do talk to some people, but they've got friends of their own. A couple of them have asked me out and stuff, but I know they've just asked because they feel sorry for me.

ASK THE EXPERTS...

Simon the social worker says...
When a close friendship cools it can be a major loss. Feeling sad is normal. **You need time to pick yourself up.** While you're feeling low you're vulnerable to being picked on and bullied by people who enjoy that sort of thing. So you might feel you ought to rush into new friendships. It's probably better to take the time to identify others you might want to be friends with – people with similar interests to you.

Anita the counsellor says...
It sounds like you're a positive person who had plenty of friends at primary school. It's hard to lose a friend and **when people are cruel, it gets you down.** It could be helpful to share your feelings with someone in your family who you are close to, or a teacher at school. Hard times don't last forever and if you start accepting invitations you will be on the way to being your old happy self again.

Mac the family liaison officer says...
Loneliness is a horrible emotion. It is even worse if people are picking on you. The first thing you need to tell yourself is that you don't deserve to be picked on, and that you shouldn't have to put up with it. Tell your parents and a teacher to get the bullying to stop. Secondly, why not say yes the next time anyone asks you out. They might not turn into a best friend, but being part of a group will make things a lot easier at school.

THE OUTCOMES

After reading our experts' advice, Owen, Lou and Jess wrote back to let us know how things turned out...

GET CONNECTED

FOLLOW THESE WEB LINKS TO FIND OUT MORE:

www.bbc.co.uk/schools/communities/onionstreet

A BBC website that offers general school advice.

www.kidscape.org.uk/childrenteens/childrenteensindex.shtml

Kidscape is a national charity set up to protect children from bullying and harm. It has good articles on making friends and starting a new school.

C A S E   S T U D Y   1

Do something positive

I realized I was feeling sorry for myself and I shouldn't have been blaming someone else for the fact that I was finding it hard to make friends. I decided to do something about it and tried out for the school football team. Some of the boys looked surprised that I'd turned up and that I could actually play. I didn't make the side but I did get talking to a couple of people and we got on okay. One of the boys was in my English class. He'd got in the team and so we just started talking about matches and stuff. He's a mate now and I've shaken off that geek image.

C A S E   S T U D Y   2

Don't give up

Cara introduced me to her friends and things just went from there. I'm still friends with Cara, even though she's not my best friend. When someone new came to our class last year, I tried to make an effort to be nice to her, because I could see she was really alone. She's not really mates with me now and that's fine because we're not really the same type of people, but I hope I made her feel a bit less lonely for a while before she found friends of her own.

> **REMEMBER**
> - If you are feeling lonely, things won't change unless you take positive action.
> - If you find making friends easy, you could help others – why not introduce them to someone you think they'd get on with.
> - There are hundreds of potential friends out there. It's up to you to find the ones you click with.
> - Smile! It's the best way to make friends.

C A S E   S T U D Y   3

Grasp opportunities

I realized that people wouldn't be inviting me out if they didn't like me. They were actually offering me friendship and I was feeling so sorry for myself I just didn't see it. So I did go out with them and we had a real laugh. I felt like my old self again. I didn't have a lot in common with some of them – they were the really clever bunch at school – but it was good to have a group to go around with. They helped me sort those other girls out too. They told me how to stand up to them, and I did! That felt great, too.

GOOD FRIENDS DO...

- Listen to you
- Include you
- Stick up for you
- Support you at difficult times
- Consider your feelings

GOOD FRIENDS DON'T...

- Talk about you behind your back
- Exclude you
- Feel jealous of you
- Expect you to spend all your time with them and no one else
- Make you feel bad about yourself

If you feel something isn't right about the way a friend behaves towards you then tell them. They might be unaware it is bothering you. If they care about your friendship, they will try to change their ways.

BEST FRIENDS
SOUL MATES OR JUST GOOD FRIENDS

For some people, having one 'best friend' is really important. Others prefer to go round with a group of friends who they also consider to be their best friends.

'I don't think boys have the "best friends" thing as much as girls.'

Being best friends is a special relationship between you and them. You know you can rely on and trust your best friends and that they are there for you when you need them. You also have the most fun with your closest friends. But what do you do when you fall out?

All friendships have their ups and downs. How you deal with problems between you depends on your personalities. It is often true that boys especially can brush arguments aside as if they never happened – there's a bust-up, you come to blows and then BOOM, it's over as quickly as it started. But then it is also often true that girls feel more intensely about their friendships and so one cross word could leave you feeling devastated.

'We are so close, we do everything together.'

When you offer someone your friendship, you hope they will value it and return the love that you show them. But what if someone doesn't value your friendship or return it in the way that you'd like? It's up to you to recognize when someone is not being a good friend. If they are making you miserable more than they are making you happy, then you need a reality check. If they are getting you into trouble or making you do things you don't want to do, it's time for a wake-up call.

8 WAYS TO DEAL WITH A BUST-UP

1 SIMMER DOWN
Leave it alone for a while, until you've both calmed down.

2 TALK CALMLY AND LISTEN
However angry you are, you need to keep your cool and talk it through, expressing your point of view and listening to theirs.

3 LEARN FROM ANY CRITICISM
If a friend criticizes your behaviour, don't immediately get **defensive.** Think about what they've said and if you think they might have a point, you can do something about it.

4 SAY SORRY
If you're in the wrong, say the words and mean them. Show how mature you can be.

5 STAND UP FOR YOURSELF
Don't be a doormat and don't apologize for living.

6 GIVE IT TIME
Some bust-ups take a little longer to heal. If you've committed a crime, you've got to do the time.

7 AGREE TO DISAGREE
If a difference of opinion has led to an argument, then agree to disagree.

8 COMPROMISE
If you can't agree on where to go or what to do or how to do something, then you need to compromise by meeting each other half way. What's more important, getting your way or keeping your friend?

13

WE FELL OUT OVER A BOY

Benita, 14, doesn't talk to her best friend anymore because she went out with the boy Benita really liked.

I really fancied this boy in my class. My best friend, Kareena, knew how I felt and I told her I was going to text him to ask him out.

> 'I knew a part of her wanted to say "yes" but she said "no" because of me. A week later she confessed that she'd been for a milkshake with him.'

She totally agreed with me, saying she thought he really liked me. But when I asked him, he said 'no'! I was really upset and embarrassed. I cried on Kareena's shoulder. A week later, the same boy asked Kareena out!

I couldn't believe it and neither could she. I knew a part of her wanted to say 'yes' but she said 'no' because of me. A week later she came in looking really chuffed with herself. She confessed that she had met up with him by accident and they'd gone for a milkshake together. She said she hadn't arranged to meet him. But loyal friends don't do that to each other. I can't bring myself to talk to her anymore.

ASK THE EXPERTS...

Simon the social worker says...
Everyone has to make their own choices. Sometimes we make the wrong ones and have to live with them. Your friend has an impossible choice. Either to take a chance of happiness and go out with this boy, hoping your friendship survives. Or to give up a chance of happiness and be miserable with you. You can make it easier for her by caring for her whatever she decides.

Anita the counsellor says...
Kareena was there for you when you were rejected by this boy. She didn't respond to him asking her out at first but couldn't say no to him in town. Could you sort things out by telling her exactly how you are feeling and giving her a chance to respond? It would be a shame if you lost your best friend over this boy and she is quite likely to be crying on your shoulder next week!

Mac the family liaison officer says...
When friendships and relationships clash, there can often be fireworks! Don't be too hard on Kareena. It sounds to me that she was trying to put you first. It's just that our emotions and our feelings towards the opposite sex can take over when we are in our teens, and even sometimes when we are grown-up. The important thing to realize is that relationships will come and go, but friendships are worth holding on to.

I'M ALWAYS THE ONE LEFT OUT

Katie, 11, has two best friends but when it comes to pairing up, she's always the one left looking for a new partner.

I have two really good friends, Chrissie and Claire. We've been best friends since Year 4.

I don't understand why it is always me who gets left out when we have to pair up in gym or in class. They just turn to one another and expect me to pair up with this other friend of ours. They also see more of one another out of school because they live close and can walk

> 'I feel really jealous of them when they do things together without me'

to one another's houses. I feel really jealous of Chrissie and Claire when they do things together without me. When Chrissie is away at her dad's, Claire always comes over to mine, but she never does when Chrissie is around. I sometimes feel they care about each other more than they do me.

ASK THE EXPERTS...

Simon the social worker says...
Your two best mates spend more time together outside school and they are closer to each other than to you. The question isn't how come you're left out so much. The question is how come your mates include you so much. There must be something about you that they really like. Think about the qualities other people see in you. If you want more friendship in your life share your special qualities and see what happens.

Anita the counsellor says...
Three is always a tricky number when it comes to friendship. If Chrissie and Claire don't notice when you get moody maybe it's time to choose a good moment and tell them that you are feeling left out sometimes. Maybe the other friend is feeling a bit used as well and you could try doing things together?

Mac the family liaison officer says...
Despite the expression, three doesn't have to be a crowd. You have all known each other for years, so there is no reason at all to think that Chrissie and Claire don't want you around. Ask them exactly why they don't always include you — you may be surprised by the answer. At the same time, do try and broaden your group of friends and you won't feel so lonely or left out if this situation happens again.

MY BEST MATE'S MOVING AWAY

'Not only am I losing my best mate, but I don't know if I'll be able to stay in the football team.'

Fred's best mate, Nick, is moving miles away. Fred's finding it difficult to imagine life without him.

When Nick told me he might have to move, I didn't really take it in. Now it's only a week away and I'm really uptight about it.

Nick and I do loads together. He's not just my school mate – most weekends he stays at mine or I stay at his and we spend most of the summer together. The other thing is that we're in this football team and his dad drives us there and back, so I'm not only losing my best mate but I don't even know if I'll be able to stay in the football team. Nothing is going to be the same. It really sucks. And I feel angry with him, but I know it's not his fault. He doesn't want to go either.

ASK THE EXPERTS...

Simon the social worker says...
Moving home brings lots of changes. Your best mate may jump at new chances, get stuck in and forget about his old life. Or he may want to talk to you about his new life and remember the past. There are lots of ways you could keep in touch if you want to, like phone, text and email. Whatever happens try thinking of this as an opportunity to make new friends.

Anita, the counsellor says...
Sounds like you are being really mature in recognizing all the different emotions you are feeling and the impact this is having on your family. Hopefully you can explain all this to your parents and the problem over the transport to football. Give yourself time to adjust and see if you can get some parental help in planning to get together with your friend in the holidays if weekends are difficult.

Mac the family liaison officer says...
Best friends can be closer to you than brothers or sisters, especially if you have known them for years. You will have loads in common and are used to spending lots of time with them, so if one of you has to move away for some reason, it's going to hurt. Talk to your parents about the football team, as losing out on this would be another blow. It also sounds like a great place to meet new friends.

THE OUTCOMES

After reading our experts' advice, Benita, Katie and Fred wrote back to let us know how things turned out...

C A S E   S T U D Y   1

Weigh it up

After I'd calmed down a bit, I told Kareena how upset she'd made me, but that I didn't want a boy to come between us. Her friendship meant much, much more to me than that. Kareena cried and said she'd been really upset when I wasn't talking to her. She said she'd never go out with him again, but I could see she really liked him. She's never had a boyfriend before – she's always been a bit shy – while I've had loads. I realized I should be happy for her ... and he has got a rather fit friend who likes me!

C A S E   S T U D Y   2

Appreciate what you have

I realize I've been looking at this all wrong. I've got two brilliant best friends and just because they live near each other it doesn't mean they like me any less. I didn't want to make an issue out of it so I didn't tell Claire or Chrissie what I'd been thinking but the next time we had to pair up in class, I did ask if I could go with one of them. They pointed out that they didn't get on so well with the girl I usually pair up with. So I guess that's the reason!

C A S E   S T U D Y   3

Think positive

It felt so unfair that Nick was moving away but there wasn't anything I could do about it, so I just had to deal with it. I spoke to Mum about football. We've only got one car and my little sister does ballet at the same time, but Mum said she'd work it out so I could still play. Sometimes the coach picks me up if I'm having trouble getting there. Nick and I text a lot but school's not the same without him. It's all right though – not as bad as I thought it was going to be. And this summer Nick's coming down for a week and I'm going up there the week after. That'll be cool.

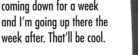

REMEMBER

• If you are feeling lonely, things won't change unless you take positive action.
• If you find making friends easy, you could help others – why not introduce them to someone you think they'd get on with?
• There are hundreds of potential friends out there. It's up to you to find the ones you click with.
• Smile! It's the best way to make friends.

17

KNOW YOURSELF

WRITE DOWN ONE DESCRIPTION FROM EACH LINE ON THE LIST BELOW THAT YOU THINK BEST SUITS YOU:

If you think you're both, write down both. And be honest with yourself – this isn't about how you would LIKE to be, it is about how you ARE.

- Outgoing or shy
- Party animal or one-on-one
- Keen to study or school's for fun
- All action or passive pursuits
- **Sensitive** soul or happy-go-lucky
- Serious or humorous
- Talkative or quiet
- Cautious or risktaker
- Lots of friends or few close friends
- Neat or scatty
- Leader or go-with-the-flow
- Think of others or keen to succeed

Now read your list. This is a general description of you. Accept it and learn to love it.

If you want to really get to know yourself better you can continue the exercise. For every negative word, think of a positive one and if there is one thing on the list you aren't happy with, try to change it.

IN WITH THE IN-CROWD
WHO'S COOL AT SCHOOL

Quite often (particularly in school) there's a definite pecking order in the friendship stakes – who's hip, who's cool, who's hot and ... who's not! But is being in with the 'in' crowd all that it's cracked up to be?

School is a great time to become part of a group, but that **doesn't mean you need to change who you are to fit in.**
By all means, move with the pack but if that means not being allowed to wear what you like or voice your own opinions, perhaps it's time to send the pack packing! Virtually everything you do, say or wear says something about how you see yourself. But it's difficult to be yourself when you think people are judging you. If you feel confident (even if it's just a front to begin with), it's more likely that people will accept you and want to spend time with you. But what if you suddenly find yourself on the outside of your crowd?

'I thought this guy was really cool. He was a goth and I guess I just copied him.'

HOW DO YOU JOIN THE IN-CROWD?

What qualifications do you need to be in with the in-crowd in your school? Is it popularity, brains, good looks, athleticism, confidence or cool clothes? Or is it **arrogance**, a narrow-mind, money, **insecurity** or **immaturity**? It depends on whether you are looking at it from the inside or the outside.

There's often one member of a group who's left out at some time or another. This can be really hard when it's you, but it's worth remembering that it will soon be someone else's turn. When you're back in, don't be tempted to join in the 'ganging up', even if you are under pressure to do so. You know how horrible it can feel and couldn't you have done with a friend who stuck up for you at the time?

'After a while I felt like a real faker.'

DARE TO BE DIFFERENT

If the pressure to fit in is getting you down, remember these five things...

1 **YOU ARE AN INDIVIDUAL**
The unique aspects of your personality or appearance may be exactly what people find appealing.

2 **DON'T CHANGE YOURSELF TO SUIT OTHERS**
If you don't be yourself, you won't feel happy or comfortable in your own skin.

3 **IT'S FINE TO BE LED, BUT DON'T BE LED ASTRAY**
Not everyone is a natural leader but trust your own judgement on what is right and wrong.

4 **OPPOSITES ATTRACT**
*Best friends can have totally opposing personalities and outlooks, but when put together they **complement** each other perfectly.*

5 **VARIETY IS THE SPICE OF LIFE**
The greater the range of friendships you have, the more interesting and varied your life will be.

HELP! I'M IN WITH A BAD CROWD

Ben, 13, has wound up in a group whose attitude he doesn't agree with. They do things that he is uncomfortable with. He wants out, but doesn't know what to do about it.

When I came **to my new school I hooked up with a boy who was really tough and fearless. He was the only person I knew and I thought it was better to be friends with him than enemies.**

He was funny and just didn't care about all the petty school rules – you could tell the teachers hated him. It was fun to start with, but then he became friends with some other boys with the same attitude and as a group we were real trouble. We'd do daft things like put the Year 6 boys in the bins and stuff. We'd always be in detention, which didn't do any good. But now they've started bullying this girl in our year. I've tried to stop them doing it but they tell me not to be such a wimp and I'm no better than they are. But I was bullied in my primary school and I hated it. I don't want to be a bully or hang around with bullies but I don't have any other friends as everyone is scared of me.

> 'He was the only person I knew and I thought it was better to be friends with him than enemies.'

ASK THE EXPERTS...

Simon the social worker says...
Having a hard reputation can come in handy. Hanging around with people who are used to getting their own way is exciting. That's okay while you feel comfortable with what's going on. When it gets too strong you know it's time to move on. So, spend time with other people too. Changing classrooms, breaktimes and queues are all chances to mix with different people.

Anita the counsellor says...
It's really good that you seem to have matured faster than this group of boys and are aware of the consequences of your actions on others. You obviously have a sense of humour which will help you to make new friends when people realize they don't have to be scared of you. Enlist support from your family or a teacher if it seems too much to handle on your own.

Mac the family liaison officer says...
There is nothing wrong with trying to be cool at your age, and being part of a tough group is bound to make you feel cooler and more grown up. However, if belonging to this group means doing things you don't want to do, and is putting off other potential friends then it is time to pull back. Try and speak to people outside the group on your own, when the rest of the gang aren't around.

I FEEL SORRY FOR HER

Tara, 14, is friendly with a girl in the school choir who she would be embarrassed to be seen with anywhere else.

'If I see her in town I pretend I haven't. I don't want her to come over and say hello.'

I am with the in-crowd, the popular group at school.

Sometimes I feel sorry for some of the others ... like this girl called Tasha who's really fat and spotty with greasy hair. She's actually really nice, but none of my crowd are interested if she's got a personality or not. I'm in the choir with her – she's the best singer in our school – but I wouldn't want to be seen with her outside of choir. If I see her in town I pretend I haven't because I don't want her to come over and say hello. Not only would my friends take the mick out of me and my 'fat choir friend', they'd probably be really nasty to her. But it's Tasha's own fault that people treat her that way. She could take more care of herself if she wanted to, couldn't she?

ASK THE EXPERTS...

Simon the social worker says...
You are obviously able to see beyond appearances. These qualities should give you some influence over your group of friends. Tasha may not necessarily come from a family who support her in caring for herself or may just not be as lucky as you are in the looks department. Sounds like you are a person who could find a way to steer your way through this tricky situation and stick up for Tasha if it's important to you.

Anita the counsellor says...
It feels good to be popular and admired. Taking care of your looks is one way to get that attention. You know pretty quickly if people like the way you look. Friendship is made of more than first impressions though. If you're confident, you can offer more to people without losing face. You can take risks and show them what you're really made of. Give yourself the chance to get to know more people better.

Mac the family liaison officer says...
When you are growing up, it is easy to worry too much about what other people think of you. You worry that if you hang around with somebody 'uncool' then you are going to become 'uncool' yourself. But you will find that if you have confidence in yourself, and be friends with who you want to be friends with, rather than who is in the 'in-crowd', then people will like you more in the long run.

I HATE WEARING MY OWN CLOTHES

Mel, 12, usually wears school uniform but on the days they are allowed to wear their own clothes she starts worrying.

'I find myself wanting to suit other people because I want to fit in.'

I hate all this labelling stuff.

I hang around with people who wouldn't mind being labelled 'townies' but if someone called me that I'd be pretty jacked off. My problem is that next week there is 'mufti day' when you get to wear your own clothes. It's really stressing me out. You see, I like wearing dresses sometimes, but if I wore some of the dresses I like, I'd get laughed at. I'd much rather wear school uniform – there's too much pressure. I find myself wanting to suit other people because I want to fit in, but then I want to be myself too and not conform to other people's likes and dislikes.

ASK THE EXPERTS...

Simon the social worker says...
I always hated 'mufti days'. I was always worried about looking cool enough and used to dread going in on the day. My advice would be don't change to fit in with any of the groups at school. If you are worried about being laughed at, maybe tone down your dress sense a little, but don't wear anything you'll feel awkward in just to try and please other people.

Anita the counsellor says...
You're right, there's certainly a lot of pressure to fit in to a category, which can cause anxiety and suppress your individuality. You are obviously a girl who has her own style and will probably be a trend leader rather than a follower when you are a bit older and more confident. In the meantime, chill out, trust your instincts and wear what you feel comfortable in.

Mac the family liaison officer says...
Although 'mufti days' sound cool, in reality they can cause problems. For people with lots of money, these days are a chance to show off the latest trendy gear, but if you don't have the latest clothes, or if you dress in a more unique or quirky way, 'mufti days' can be a worry. My advice would be wear just what you want to wear and don't change or try to impress anyone. There will be plenty of others feeling the same way as you.

THE OUTCOMES

After reading our experts' advice, Ben, Tara and Mel wrote back to let us know how things turned out...

CASE STUDY 1

Be brave

I decided I was more bothered by going along with what my mates were doing than I was by being on my own. I just stopped going around with them, making excuses that I had to be somewhere else. They soon got the message and didn't bother with me anymore. It's funny because then one of the other boys in the group, Taz, came and found me one lunchtime. He never said so but I think he was feeling the same as me. Now we hang around together and we've made other mates too. I'm much happier – and things are better at home because I'm not getting into so much trouble.

GET CONNECTED

FOLLOW THIS WEB LINK TO FIND OUT MORE:

www.youngminds.org.uk/youngpeople/index.php

A website dedicated to looking after the mental health of young people. Good for information on everything from anxiety to depression.

CASE STUDY 2

Do the right thing

I know I was being really unfair to Tasha but I didn't have a lot of sympathy for her because she didn't do anything about her appearance. We had a school concert and we all had to dress up in white and black outfits. Tasha actually made an effort! I told her she looked good and that she should do her hair like that all the time. I know it's wrong to be embarrassed to be seen with Tasha. She is nice and now all my friends know that I like her. If I see her in town, I go over to her to say hello. It's better that way – for Tasha especially.

CASE STUDY 3

Stop worrying

I was thinking far too much about it and was having this big battle in my head. I knew it wasn't worth losing sleep over but I couldn't help it. I decided to wear clothes I like and those I feel good in, but nothing that would make me stand out. I'll keep my dresses for when I go out with my family! I'm not going to dress to impress – that's SO not me – but I do like to fit in and not have people laugh at me all the time.

REMEMBER

- No one is better than anyone else. We're just different and we all have our good and bad points.
- It's normal to want to fit in but change only if YOU want to, not to please others.
- Aim to be happy in yourself rather than wanting to be someone else.
- Respect people's differences and you will earn respect yourself.

GREEN-EYED MONSTER
Jealousy can lead to cruelty

Being jealous is when you envy what someone else has. It can be an extremely destructive emotion, and is often the motivation behind bullying.

Everyone feels jealous at some time in their lives. If you have an older brother or sister who seems to get more attention from your parents than you do, or if you have a best friend who constantly hogs the limelight, then you are sure to have had an attack of the green-eyed monster at some time. Jealousy can be a positive force, making you look at your own life and think how you can make it better. However, it can also be a very negative emotion. If you dislike somebody just because they are more popular, attractive or successful than you, you might end up focusing all your energies on this person rather than on achieving your own goals. Many bullies are driven by jealousy.

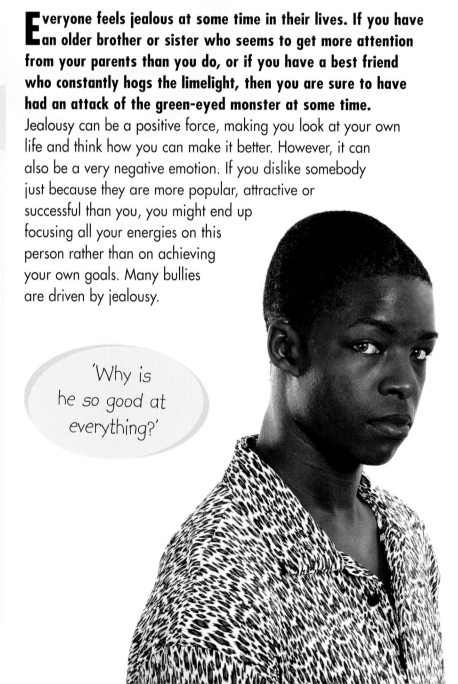

'Why is he so good at everything?'

10 REASONS FOR JEALOUSY

YOU MIGHT FEEL JEALOUS OF OTHERS IF THEY:

- Are more popular
- Are more intelligent
- Are more talented
- Are more attractive
- Are funnier
- Are kinder
- Have nicer clothes
- Have nicer possessions
- Have more style
- Have more money

Do you ever feel jealous about one of the above? Instead of worrying about what other people have, concentrate on your own good points. Make a list of 10 things that are good about you!

I'M THE JEALOUS ONE. WHAT CAN I DO?

Jealousy is a sign of insecurity. It indicates a lack of confidence on your part. Acting in a jealous fashion will push friends away. Instead, try to have confidence in yourself and your own abilities.

Their lack of confidence and **insecurity** generates envy, which in turn is expressed in the form of anger towards others. Jealous people can target people for being better looking, more intelligent, more popular, and countless other reasons.

If they see someone with something that they don't have, they try to take it away from them through the use of violence or verbal bullying. Remember if a jealous person is picking on you, that what they are doing is bullying. They are seeking to destroy your confidence to bring you down to their level. Always remember that jealousy is never an excuse for bullying others, and in the end simply drives people away.

'He makes snide remarks all the time.'

6 WAYS TO DEAL WITH A GREEN-EYED MONSTER

What should you do if someone is jealous of you?

1 **KEEP YOUR SELF-ESTEEM**
Remember all your good qualities. You are a good and talented person, so don't let the jealous person knock your self-esteem by convincing you otherwise.

2 **WALK AWAY**
Don't get into a debate with a jealous person. You don't have to justify yourself and the skills and abilities you have.

3 **STAND UP FOR YOURSELF**
A jealous bully likes to pick on less confident people. Stand up for yourself and have confidence and they will back off.

4 **TALK IT THROUGH**
Talk to a friend about what is going on. Never suffer in silence.

5 **TELL SOMEONE**
Always tell a teacher or another adult you trust if a jealous person is picking on you.

6 **FIND OTHER FRIENDS**
People who are jealous of you aren't real friends. Good friends are happy for you when you are doing well!

• GReeN-eyeD MONSTeR •

I ALWAYS COME SECOND

Lorna, 13, and her friend Amy started entering modelling competitions together. They both love it, but Amy is so pretty she usually wins, which leaves Lorna feeling envious and upset.

My friend Amy and I saw a modelling competition in a girl's magazine. You had to send in photos of yourself with a friend. We couldn't believe it when they called us up to go for a photoshoot.

We enjoyed it so much that we now enter every competition but Amy's really, really pretty and she always wins. And I usually come second...or nowhere. Her family is rich and she always has great clothes. It's so hard not to be jealous, but she's my friend and I never say

anything. Inside, though, I know how I feel. When she wins, she asks me, 'Are you okay?' She isn't being nasty, she's being nice, but I wish, just once, that I'd win instead. She says she's jealous of me because I'm prettier, but I actually think she just has more confidence and the right clothes.

> 'It's so hard not to be jealous, but she's my friend and I never say anything. Inside, though, I know how I feel.'

ASK THE EXPERTS...

Simon the social worker says...
Jealousy isn't a very helpful feeling. First, you find out you're not as good as you thought you were. Then, along comes jealousy to tell you there's someone else better than you. It's like being slapped in the face twice! The truth is though, there is no need to feel jealous. No one is better than you. You are unique and have lots of special qualities to offer. Try not to compare yourself to others and you should be much happier.

Anita the counsellor says...
You certainly are a good friend to be able to express yourself without a word of criticism of Amy. It must be really hard to lose out to her so regularly. There's no need to feel bad about being jealous. Try to hear what Amy is saying to you about envying your good looks! Your confidence will develop in time and your ability to be a good friend is far more important than how you look.

Mac the family liaison officer says...
Having a really glamorous friend who always seems to come first at everything can be a real pain. But only if you let it be. I am sure that Amy has no idea that her success would be bothering you in this way, and would probably be really upset about it if she knew. Rather than measuring yourself against Amy, see if you can learn with her and boost your own **self-esteem.**

MY MUM AND DAD ARE USELESS

Rachel, 12, gets jealous of her friends because they have great holidays and get new clothes all the time.

I'm quite jealous of my friends, but just in a lightweight way – I wish I was as good-looking as her, or I wish I made boys laugh like her.

But I don't think it's ever got to the stage where it's eating away at me. I do get jealous about money though – my parents are always skint! We can't afford holidays to Florida or to buy new clothes all the time, which some of my friends can do. That really gets to me, and I get so fed up with my parents for being so useless. My dad works but he doesn't earn a lot of money. I don't understand why he can't get a better job – he just doesn't try. And my mum could work too. She looks after my two brothers, but she could do child-minding to bring in more money.

> 'I do get jealous about money – my parents are always skint.'

ASK THE EXPERTS...

Simon the social worker says...
We don't choose our parents. As you get older you start to see their faults. It's a sign you're growing up and thinking for yourself. Measuring them against other people's parents won't get you any further though. Your parents made their own choices. They won't change just because you don't approve. If money's short you need to get out there and earn some yourself!

Anita the counsellor says...
You're doing well not to let jealousy seriously get to you. Your parents have obviously managed to raise a son who relates well to others and keeps things in perspective. Although it must be disappointing not to have as much money as some of your friends, try not to blame your parents. They are most likely doing their best for you and your brothers.

Mac the family liaison officer says...
I don't think any teenager thinks their parents are cool! I remember when I was growing up cringing at the things my Mum and Dad did, when everyone else's parents seemed much cooler and knew what their kids wanted. The thing to remember is that your parents really do love you and they always try to do their best for you. Try and remember this when you feel down.

CASE STUDY 3

I FEEL LIKE A STUNTED DWARF

Matt, 15, found it hard when his friend Toby suddenly turned into a Greek god when he still looked like a kid.

My best mate at primary school really started annoying me when we got to secondary school. He shot up in height all of a sudden.

His voice broke much earlier than mine. Suddenly he was like a Greek god and I was still this stunted dwarf next to him. He is now the tallest and oldest-looking boy in our year and all the girls fancy him. All I get is, 'Ah, look at little Matt.'

He's just got so up himself, saying things like, 'Don't worry, Matt, you'll get a girlfriend … one day.' He isn't really rubbing my face in it, but he always talks about his latest sports trophy or his latest 'A' and I feel really bad about myself. It makes me not want to spend time with him because I feel really inadequate in his company.

> 'It makes me not want to spend time with him because I feel really inadequate in his company.'

ASK THE EXPERTS...

Simon the social worker says...
At primary school it doesn't matter too much what you look like. At secondary school that changes and there's pressure to be attractive. But everyone grows and matures at their own speed. There's no knowing when, or how you'll turn out. Instead of worrying about what you haven't got think about all your good points. Think about your strengths and build on them.

Anita the counsellor says...
Maybe you and your best friend have grown apart in more ways than one!
Everyone grows up at their own rate and height is not the only way of measuring maturity. You are able to express your feelings honestly and this is just as likely to bring you success with girls in the future as your mate's method of blowing his own trumpet.

Mac the family liaison officer says...
When we hit our teens, we develop at different rates. Some boys hit puberty as early as 11, while for others it doesn't happen until much later. Don't measure yourself against Toby. Be patient, and in time you will start to grow yourself. In the meantime, hanging around with a 'Greek god' will bring you into contact with lots of girls – which means more potential girlfriends!

THE OUTCOMES

After reading our experts' advice, Lorna, Rachel and Matt wrote back to let us know how things turned out...

GET CONNECTED

**FOLLOW THIS
WEB LINK
TO FIND OUT MORE:**

www.teengrowth.com

A health website that offers information and advice on puberty, family, friends, drugs, sex and emotions.

CASE STUDY 1

Control the monster

I know how I feel is wrong. It's not as if I want to feel jealous of Amy. I want to be happy for her because she's my friend and she's so pretty that she could be a model when she's older. It's just that I want to be, too. My stepmum says that I should feel proud of myself for coming second in competitions – I'm up against loads of pretty girls, not just Amy. I've also heard that modelling agencies don't always go for the prettiest girls anyway, sometimes they want more unusual looks. So maybe there's a place for both Amy and I up there on the catwalk. You never know.

CASE STUDY 2

Think it through

I feel bad about saying that about my parents. The last holiday we had was really good fun – we went with my cousins and we went climbing, which was great. I can't help feeling jealous of my friends when they get stuff. Dad suggested I get a paper round, but I could never get up that early. No way.

CASE STUDY 3

Don't give up on yourself

I've filled out a bit now and I've had girlfriends, so now it's not such a big deal. I knew, deep down, I was just jealous and that Toby couldn't do anything to change things, but I just couldn't help myself. He's always been a good mate and it wasn't his fault that I felt inadequate around him. It doesn't matter now. I'm no Greek god, but my voice has broken now and I suppose I get to meet more girls because Toby is such a babe magnet!

REMEMBER
• If you are feeling jealous, try and think about your own qualities and what a good person you are.
• If someone is picking on you because they are envious of you, don't keep quiet. Tell someone!
• Jealousy is the problem of the person who feels jealous. It is never your fault!

WHAT REASONS DO YOUR PARENTS HAVE FOR DISLIKING YOUR FRIENDS?

- You always get into trouble when you're with them.
- They don't like the way your friends look.
- They think your friend is disrespectful and rude.
- They have formed an opinion based on religion, race, wealth or social status.
- They have issues with your friend's parents, and what they allow your friend to do.
- They do not feel that your friend treats you properly.

Ask yourself, are their issues reasonable or unreasonable?

Very often your parents are simply trying to protect you from potential **conflict** *or harm, but sometimes their opinions are totally unjustified. You need to find a way to convince your parents of your friend's good qualities.*

PARENT POWER
WHEN PARENTS AND FRIENDS DON'T GET ON

So your mum hates your mate or won't let your friends come over. What do you do?

Parental disapproval of your pals can be very trying at times. They will give you such a hard time, if they think you have 'got in with a bad lot'.

It's usually fair to say that parents make their decisions because they care about you and want to keep you safe. They rely on their own experiences to make judgements, but their experiences aren't exactly the same as yours, and they have a tendency to imagine the worst! It's up to you to be mature about it.

'My mum is such a snob.'

Understanding why a parent has reacted so badly to one friend and not to others is a good way to start solving the problem. If you really can't see their point of view, talk to them about it (not shout!) and tell them why they are wrong.

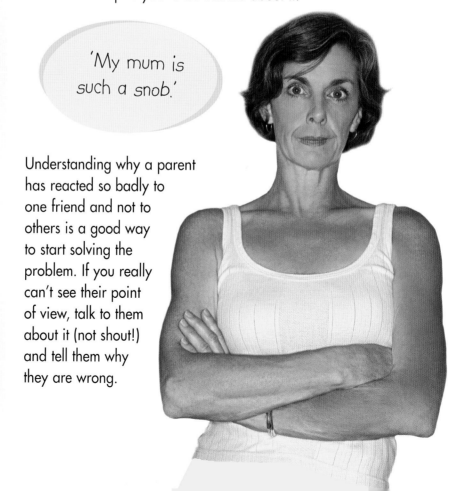

'Why won't they let me be friends with who I want to be with?'

Another big problem with parents is if they won't let you have your friends over, or if they embarrass you when your friends do come over! Worse still is if they treat your friends badly or make them feel uncomfortable. If you find it hard to talk to your parents about it, then maybe there is someone else who can help, such as a grandparent, godparent or family friend. Yes, it is their house and you need to abide by their rules to keep the peace, but if they are upsetting you, you need to find a way to reason with them.

6 WAYS TO DEAL WITH A BUST-UP

Here are some tips for dealing with parents:

1 BE RESPONSIBLE
Show them you can be trusted to make your own judgements and act responsibly. They will be more likely to let you do the things that you want to do.

2 DO A DEAL
If you want to get your own way about something, try **negotiating** terms before the event.

3 COVER ALL THE ANGLES
Think about any objections they may have to something before asking. Then prepare yourself to respond reasonably and sensibly.

4 DON'T LIE
Parents aren't stupid. If you lie to them and get found out, you'll lose their trust.

5 TALK IT THROUGH
Any issue you may have in your home life is best solved by talking. Don't hide things from your parents (including your feelings).

6 REMEMBER IT'S TWO-WAY
It's not all about what you want. Show that you are keen to do things for your parents, and they'll be far more willing to do things for you.

MY FRIEND GOT THE BLAME

Belle, 14, was caught shoplifting with her friend, Suzette. Her dad immediately blamed Suzette. But it was Belle's fault too.

Me and my mate got caught shoplifting and Dad straightaway blamed it on my friend, Suzette.

The thing is, it wasn't just her – it was both of us. We just didn't think about it, and we didn't think what happened would happen. We'd never done it before. We had the money and wanted to buy these bits for our hair. They were so little and we were in a rush. We both looked at each other and just did it. Then we got caught and arrested and it was awful. Suzette doesn't live near me and so I was staying over with her family, which is why I think Dad blamed her even more. We had to go to the police station and were there for the whole day – it was so awful and horrible. Dad wouldn't talk to me for a whole week and I've got a record until I'm 16. Dad won't let me speak to Suzette on the phone. I'm scared to ring her because I think she'll hate me now. It wasn't like it was more her fault than mine – she was the one crying when it happened. I was just so in shock.

> 'He shouted down the phone at her and won't let me call her from home anymore.'

ASK THE EXPERTS...

Simon the social worker says...
You and your friend made a mistake. You didn't stop each other from stealing. **And your dad has decided you aren't good for each other.** It will take time to show him you are not going to lose your self-control like that again. You might be able to speed things up by staying calm with him and talking to him about it. Show him you're in control of yourself and that you've thought things through.

Anita the counsellor says...
This sounds like a really upsetting incident for everybody involved and, like you, your dad is finding ways to cope with it. When he has calmed down a bit try to talk to him about it and explain what actually happened and how upset Suzette was. It will take a while to earn your dad's trust again and show him you have learnt from the experience.

Mac the family liaison officer says...
When we are young, the **need to fit in can sometimes lead us into dangerous situations.** I think you both realize that you have done something that you shouldn't have, but it is going to take a while to convince your dad that you are really sorry. Give it time, and maybe in the future he will let you speak to Suzette from home, once he realizes that this event was a one off for both of you.

**FOLLOW THESE
WEB LINKS
TO FIND OUT MORE:**

www.bbc.co.uk/schools/
communities/onionstreet

A BBC website that offers general
school advice.

www.kidscape.org.uk/
childrenteens/
childrenteensindex.shtml

Kidscape is a national charity
set up to protect children
from bullying and harm.
It has good articles
on making friends
and starting a
new school.

THE OUTCOME

After reading our experts' advice, Belle wrote back to let us know how things turned out...

C A S E   S T U D Y

Be truthful

My dad has always thought of me as his perfect little girl (which really annoys my brother!) but I couldn't let him carry on blaming Suzette for something that was my fault, too. He started telling other parents how bad she was and it wasn't right. So I told him that I'd been the one who first thought of doing it and that Suzette had gone along with it. It was a bit of a lie,

but I didn't care – it was the only thing that would really shut him up about it. The most **hypocritical** thing is that Dad then admitted that he'd nicked stuff when he was a kid! But he wasn't caught. I knew Dad would never apologize to Suzette for shouting at her but he did back off. Suzette and I meet up in town still, but we'd never do anything stupid again. I still go to her house, but she never comes to mine. She doesn't want to, and I don't blame her. It would just be awkward for everyone.

REMEMBER

Most parents or carers –
though not all, it is true – have the
best interests of their children at heart.
So although it may feel like it, they are not
just trying to spoil your fun. They are concerned
about you and are doing their best to protect you
from being hurt. They are also responsible for you
and so if you get into trouble it may make them feel
like they've failed. Equally, your parents or carers need
to know that you are responsible enough for them to let
go and recognize that you are growing up. It's a cruel
fact of life that most of us have to learn from our own
mistakes, and most parents do realize this as much as
they might not want to admit it.

But if your parents are being unreasonable,
you need to talk to them. If they don't like your
friends, tell them what you like about them.
Sell them to your parents and try to make
them see your point of view. If you still
don't get anywhere, leave it alone
and keep the two separate –
for your sanity's sake.

THE FRIENDSHIP TEST

OLD FRIENDS

- Know you inside out
- Know your family
- Can rely on and trust each other
- Can get jealous of new friendships

NEW FRIENDS

- Are exciting
- Offer opportunities to try new things
- May have more in common with you
- May not be true friends

It's all too easy to neglect old friends, when you move to a new school or meet a new group of people, but beware – your new friendships might not last and your old friends might not be there to pick up the pieces.

FRIENDS FOR LIFE?
IF IT'S TIME TO MOVE ON

Some people are friends from the first day of primary school through to old age, although this is rare. But what do you do when your friendship starts to fade?

You might be best friends with someone right now who you couldn't imagine not being friends with in the future, but it could happen. As you get older, move schools, move house, meet other people – your friendship could fade. But don't sweat it if you are losing contact with a friend. It's not the end of the world and there will be other friends round the corner to take their place. It's not so easy, though, if only one of you wants to let the friendship fizzle out.

'We've got nothing in common anymore.'

As ever, communication is the way to deal with the problem. Have a think about how you feel and work out what you want to say, then say it. You may both need a little time to think about what is important to you, or to come to terms with the fact that the friendship might be over.

'She really annoys me.'

It will be awkward afterwards, but someone has to bite the bullet and face facts. But what do you do if someone wants to be your friend who you'd sooner crawl through a swamp than hang out with? Just saying you've got to go or you've made other plans may or may not work, depending on their character. If they are **sensitive**, they'll probably see immediately that they are not wanted. But if they are thick-skinned, you're going to have to toughen up, too, and let them directly know that you don't want to spend time with them. Think about how you'd like to be dumped – kindly, right? So be nice, and if that's not an option, be fair. It's not necessary to be rude or cruel – however annoying they are!

5 GOOD WAYS TO DITCH A FRIEND... KINDLY!

You realize that it's time for a parting of the ways. How do you move on without hurting his or her feelings?

1 DON'T KEEP IN TOUCH
The easiest way to split is just to stop calling or texting.

2 FOCUS ON YOUR NEW INTERESTS
Quite often, the reason that friendships dissolve is that you no longer feel you have anything in common. By focusing more time on your new passions, you will probably find that your friend will do likewise.

3 HONESTY IS THE BEST POLICY
If friends want to spend more time with you than you want to spend with them, be honest with them.

4 HELP THEM TO MOVE ON
Encourage your friend to make new friends and to do new things with their life. As they broaden their friendship circles, they'll become less dependent on you.

5 ACCEPT THAT PEOPLE CHANGE
*Just because you always thought you'd remain lifelong friends, it doesn't necessarily mean that you will. As your circumstances and **aspirations** change, so may your friends' and ultimately you may just grow apart. It's natural.*

WE'RE NOT MATES ANYMORE

Nicko, 13, and his friend Abs now go to different schools and they have both found new friends. Their friendship is fizzling out but it seems to be mutual.

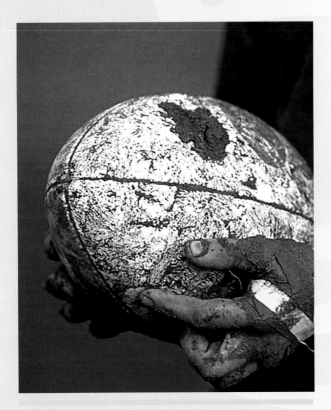

My mate, Abs, passed his 11+ and went to a grammar school a couple of years ago.

We live really near each other and play in the local football team, so we stayed friends for ages. Then he started playing rugby and cricket and he lost interest in football. I'd see him in town with boys who looked and behaved like such jerks – really up themselves and snobby.

Abs hasn't changed and we still get on well, but we don't see so much of each other. I do feel a bit funny about it but all my new mates are into football and girls – not rugby and homework, which is what Abs always seems to be doing.

> 'Abs hasn't changed and we still get on well, but we don't see so much of each other.'

ASK THE EXPERTS...

Simon the social worker says...
Sometimes everything works out when best friends go their different ways. So when something changes in your life like this and everything goes well it's a good idea to ask yourself a couple of questions. What was it that helped you handle the situation? How did you manage to do that so well? If you always think about your worries you won't notice your happiness and success.

Anita the counsellor says...
Everyone goes through changes as they get older and you seem to be confident **that the choices you have made are right for you.** It's good to hear that you and Abs are still able to spend some time together and accept each other as you are, even though you now have new friends of your own with common interests.

Mac the family liaison officer says...
Friendships change as we get older. It is unrealistic to think we'll keep the same sets of friends throughout our lives. Don't cut Abs off totally, but don't try to force a friendship that seems to be fading if you don't really have that much in common anymore.

CASE STUDY

THE OUTCOME

After reading our experts' advice, Nicko wrote back to let us know how things turned out...

C A S E   S T U D Y

Accept change

Now when I see Abs we just say 'hi' and that's that. He's got his own friends now and I've got mine. I don't see the point of pretending and it seems to have worked out okay. It's funny to think that I was worried about going to secondary school without Abs. I met up with people in the first week who I seemed to have much more in common with. I don't know if Abs and I will become good friends again in the future. Maybe we will, maybe we won't. It doesn't matter now. He's having a good time and so am I.

GET CONNECTED

FOLLOW THESE WEB LINKS TO FIND OUT MORE:

www.bbc.co.uk/ schools/communities/onionstreet

A BBC website that offers general school advice.

www.kidscape.org.uk/ childrenteens/ childrenteensindex.shtml

Kidscape is a national charity set up to protect children from bullying and harm. It has good articles on making friends and starting a new school.

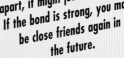

REMEMBER
- Few friends last a lifetime – sad but true. Keep your self-respect at all times.
- If someone is trying to shake you off, walk away. It's their loss.
- Treat others as you would like to be treated. Being rude or cruel is NEVER necessary. Don't turn friends into enemies. Old friends can make the very worst enemies, so try to stay friendly even if you're not spending time with each other.
- If you and a friend are drifting apart, it might just be a phase. If the bond is strong, you may be close friends again in the future.

IT'S A BOY/ GIRL THING

FRIENDS OF THE OPPOSITE SEX

Can you have a friend of the opposite sex without being romantically linked? Of course you can ... as long as it's mutual.

Being good friends with a person of the opposite gender with no romantic feelings involved is called a 'platonic' friendship. You love to hang out together, you feel totally relaxed in each other's company, but you have no urge to snog because you're just great mates.

Platonic friendships can be long-lasting and just as valuable as a friendship with someone of your own sex. Platonic friends can give you a different angle on life. Generally the opposite sex have different interests, priorities and ways of seeing things.

'Boys can't be friends with girls. They always fancy them underneath.'

There's also the added benefit of being able to discuss the mysteries of the opposite sex with a person with inside knowledge. It's often the case that as soon as you become interested in the opposite sex you realize how little you know about them. There is nothing quite like having a friend of the same age who has all the answers about boy or girl behaviour because they happen to be one. Plus, they usually have some pretty fit friends they can introduce you to! But having a friend of the opposite sex can also be misunderstood by your other friends. Another problem is jealousy.

THE ULTIMATE GIRL MATE

- She's the girl who you can be stupid with but doesn't make you feel stupid.
- She's the girl you can talk to without flirting.
- She's the girl who tells you who is right for you and who isn't.
- She's the girl who tells you where you are going wrong but who never sounds like she's **criticizing** you.

THE ULTIMATE BOY MATE

- He's the boy whose shoulder you can cry on.
- He's the boy who you don't mind seeing when you're looking your worst.
- He's the boy you can talk to about anything.
- He's the boy who really makes you laugh but you don't fancy.
- He's the boy who looks out for you and points you in the right direction when it comes to dating.

When you go out with people romantically,
they may not accept your boy or gal pal. If you
always go around with people of the opposite sex,
it could also lead to taunts about your sexuality.
Hopefully you'll be able to deal with it effectively or not let
it bother you – it's probably the very reason why you prefer not to
hang around with your own sex anyway! If you've got good friends, they will back you up.
But if it is bothering you or if it gets serious, talk to a school counsellor or teacher about it.
Like all relationships, girl/boy friendships can have their difficulties, but it is fair to say that
a boy who is good friends with a girl, and a girl who is good
friends with a boy is all the richer for it.

> 'He's got so many female friends he must be gay.'

BUT I'M FALLING IN LOVE WITH HER. WHAT CAN I DO?

Sometimes platonic friendships can turn into something more, but crossing the line between friend and date can be a risky business. You could end up losing someone special just because you were curious about kissing them. If you take the risk and it turns out to be a mistake, hopefully it may even strengthen the bond between you.

JUST GOOD FRIENDS

Claire, 14, has been friends with Matt since starting secondary school. They don't meet up much but they're always texting. Now he's asked her out and she doesn't know how to deal with it.

Matt and I were in the same form when we were about 11. We now go to different schools but we still text all the time.

I don't know why he's suddenly asked me out. He's never shown any interest in me before in that way. He's always been keen on pretty, quiet girls – quite the opposite of me. I think he's just feeling like he wants to have a girlfriend because his mates all do. I'm going to have to tell him that I just want to stay friends. I've never looked at him that way, and I don't think I ever could. I'm sure he's going to be cool with it. I hope he is anyway because I don't want it to ruin our friendship.

> 'I think he's just feeling like he wants to have a girlfriend because his mates all do.'

ASK THE EXPERTS...

Simon the social worker says...
It's great when two people can talk to each other about their friendship. You say what you think and you learn something new about each other. Then you can choose if what you've told each other can bring you closer. Or if you'd be better off further apart. It's a good idea to talk like this whenever you think things might change. Keep talking to each other and keep your friendship alive.

Anita the counsellor says...
It's nice to hear that you and Matt have enjoyed a good friendship and that you have some idea where he's coming from. You sound very sensible in wanting to let him know how you feel about his invitation as soon as possible. My guess would be that knowing him so well will help you let him down gently while trying to maintain your friendship.

Mac the family liaison officer says...
This could be a tricky situation, but not if you tread carefully. Tell him the truth – that you really treasure and value his friendship, but that you think it would spoil things to become boyfriend and girlfriend. You might even find he is relieved when you tell him this. Sometimes when all your mates are getting boyfriends and girlfriends, there is great pressure to follow suit, even if your heart isn't really in it.

IT'S A FAMILY THING

Harvey and Tilda, now 14, have been friends for years. Apart from a snog a couple of years ago, there's nothing more between them. But Harvey has a girlfriend and she's getting jealous.

> 'My mates started teasing me but eventually they got bored.'

I've been friends with Tilda for years. Our families are friends so we've even been on holiday together. We don't go to the same school so we have to make an effort to meet up.

There was a phase when we were younger and everyone was getting into the boy/girl thing and my mates started teasing me, saying, 'You fancy her. You love her.' I didn't react and eventually they got bored. Everyone knows that Tilda and I are just good friends. We did have one sneaky snog when we were about 11, but it was just to see what it was like. I have had girlfriends who are a bit weird about it, but my latest girlfriend is getting really jealous. Why can't she just accept that Tilda's a friend?

ASK THE EXPERTS...

Simon the social worker says...
Old friends and family friends are special. They probably know more about you than most of your school friends. Keeping these relationships going may be difficult especially if they are friends of the opposite sex. You may not see them as often as you see people at school and your regular mates may not have a history with them. But having different friends in different areas of life makes things more interesting.

Anita the counsellor says...
I'm not surprised that your present girlfriend is having trouble getting her head around the fact that you and Tilda are just good friends. The fact that you have such long and close shared history could be quite a threat, or it may be that your girlfriend is lacking confidence in herself. Listen to her fears and reassure her but don't let her anxiety stop you from being true to yourself.

Mac the family liaison officer says...
Sometimes when a couple start having a relationship, one of them thinks that this means they shouldn't need any other friends. This is a big mistake, however, as at this age, relationships don't last for long. Tell your girlfriend that you have been friends with Tilda for years, that there is no reason on earth to be jealous, and that you wouldn't try to stop her having her own friends.

CASE STUDY 3

HE'S FALLEN IN LOVE WITH ME

Mandy, 14, hangs around with boys more than girls but now one of the boys says he's in love with her...

I find girls quite bitchy. I know I can be bitchy myself, but some girls are super bitchy and hard to get along with. I tend to hang around boys more. They can be a good laugh and I quite often think they are the best friends to have.

The trouble is that this one boy, Tad, says he's fallen in love with me. I don't feel the same way so I've ended up hurting him. A lot of stuff has gone on and it has just ruined our friendship. It's also meant that when Tad's

around the other boys find it awkward inviting me places, so I'm the one left behind. It's not really fair because I didn't ask Tad to fall in love with me. Now I'm worried about being friends with other boys just in case the same thing happens. It's just too awkward and embarrassing and I hate hurting people's feelings.

> 'A lot of stuff has gone on and it has ruined our friendship.'

ASK THE EXPERTS...

Simon the social worker says...
However hard you try it isn't always possible to make everything okay for other people. It isn't your job to look after them. Only they can sort their own feelings out anyway. All you can do is what seems best for you at the time, while respecting the other person's feelings. And if anything like this happens to you or one of your friends in the future you'll probably have a better idea of what to do.

Anita the counsellor says...
Good for you for being a kind person who respects others feelings. Maybe if you talk to Tad and the others the situation will be able to move forward. Try not to be down about how things have turned out this time. You are bound to have learnt something about picking up the signs that someone is falling for you. This will help you handle a similar situation in the future.

Mac the family liaison officer says...
It sounds to me as if your friend is the one at fault.
Tell him that it really isn't on for him to make you feel awkward around your friends. Don't stop making friends with boys in the future. This situation may well happen again, but provided you communicate how you feel to your friends and be conscious not to send out the wrong signals to your mates then things should turn out okay.

THE OUTCOMES

After reading our experts' advice, Claire, Harvey and Mandy told us how things turned out...

CASE STUDY 1

Trust your judgement

I was right. Matt was cool with it. It didn't change our friendship a bit. I knew he wouldn't talk about me behind my back or judge me for anything I did. We text as much as ever now and in a way I feel even closer to him than I did before – like we've got something a bit special and we understand each other. Another good thing is that he's just invited me to his school disco. He goes to an all-boys school and so he wants me to bring some girls. Secretly, I think he fancies my friend, but that's fine by me because I fancy his!

CASE STUDY 2

Keep it real

It was more my girlfriend's problem than mine and it really put me off. I'd been honest and upfront about Tilda and she still couldn't say, 'Okay, I trust you,' so she ended up being a total pain in the neck. I do talk to Tilda in a different way to my mates. I ask her for advice on stuff that I wouldn't ask them. Like, I asked her what to wear to meet this one girl, and with this other girl who she knew, I asked whether she liked cocky guys, like me! And she's asked me about stuff, like 'Why do boys do that?' about gross stuff. But what can I say? Boys are just gross!

CASE STUDY 3

Put it down to experience

Things were awkward for a while, but the boys didn't put up with Tad's moping for long. They told him to get over it and I think he is trying to. When we're out we just don't really talk to one another. There are enough of us in our group to be able to do that. I think he's still hoping that I'm going to change my mind one day, but I won't – I just don't fancy him and I never will. He needs to find someone else and the sooner the better.

GET CONNECTED

FOLLOW THESE WEB LINKS TO FIND OUT MORE:

www.childrens-express.org

A news site for young people with articles by young people.

www.kidzworld.com

Site with advice, games and chat for young people.

REMEMBER
- It's up to you who you are friends with.
- If your feelings change, it's best to be honest.
- Having a boy or gal pal is just as rewarding as other friendships – and sometimes more long-lasting.

43

GREAT MATE OR FICKLE FRIEND?

Test how you rate as a mate by following this flow chart...

START HERE

You get a text from your mate. Do you let them wait a while before you reply?

NO

Do you always forget your mates' birthdays?

NO

Your mate's being bullied. Do you stand up to the bully or tell someone else?

YES

YES

Your mate's gone mad with the fake tan. He or she is saying it's natural. Do you blow their cover?

NO

Your mate tries on a top that looks awful on them. Do you tell them so?

YES

YES

YES

NO

She/he's got a new crush and does nothing but go on about it. Do you tell her/him to shut up or ship out?

NO

YES

NO

Do you ever make your friend the butt of your jokes?

NO

Your mate tells you something they are really embarrassed about. Do you tell any of your other friends?

NO

You're engrossed in your fave TV programme. The phone rings and it's your mate. Do you arrange to ring them back later?

YES

NO

YES

NO

NO

Your mate's having a really bad hair day. Do you laugh?

YES

Can you see an end to your friendship with your best mate?

NO

Have you ever got together with your mate's crush?

YES

YES

44

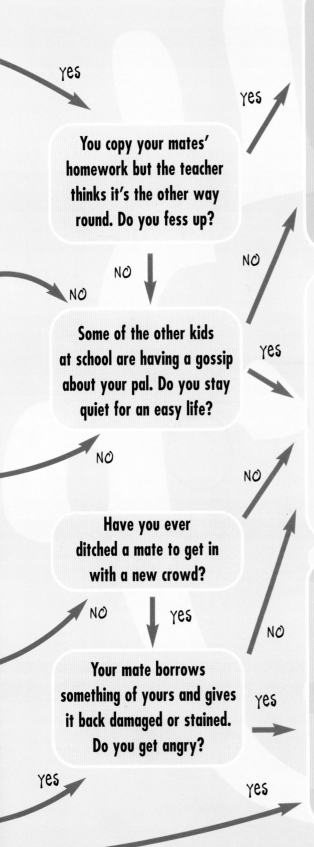

yes

You copy your mates' homework but the teacher thinks it's the other way round. Do you fess up?

yes

NO

NO

NO

Some of the other kids at school are having a gossip about your pal. Do you stay quiet for an easy life?

yes

NO

NO

NO

Have you ever ditched a mate to get in with a new crowd?

NO   yes

Your mate borrows something of yours and gives it back damaged or stained. Do you get angry?

yes

yes

NO

yes

yes

PERFECT PAL

You've certainly got what it takes to make it as a top mate. You usually know just the right thing to say and you'll always be there for a friend in need. You're willing to compromise and you have your friend's best interests at heart. At the same time you won't be trampled all over and are happy to stand up for what you believe is right. You're loyal, dependable and fun to be around. Your mates are lucky to have you as a friend!

FAITHFUL FRIEND

You tend to let others walk all over you and you don't stand up for yourself. You can be a loyal friend and often put others' needs before your own. Maybe your friends are more dominant, but if you have the confidence to stand up and be yourself, other people will respect and like you for it. It's good to be unselfish, but it doesn't harm to be assertive once in a while. Good for you for being such a sweetie ... but make sure you get something in return.

ROTTEN MATE

With friends like you, who needs enemies! You have a lot to learn about friendships. Are you aware that your mates have feelings too, or does the whole universe revolve around you? In your opinion, it's a dog-eat-dog world and you've got to be selfish to get anywhere in life. It's good to go after what you want but you're missing how valuable friends are in helping you achieve your goals. If you carry on as you are, the only friend you'll have is you!

ARROGANCE *having a high, often overinflated, opinion of yourself. Feeling you have superiority over others.*

ASPIRATIONS *things you want to achieve in life*

COMPLEMENT *add to, enhance or complete something. Someone who complements you is a person whose personality balances well with yours, so when working together your combined strengths and abilities are greater than your individual efforts would be. (Not to be confused with 'compliment', which means to flatter.)*

COMPROMISE *settling a dispute by both giving a bit to the other. Meeting half way.*

CONFLICT *being at odds with something. To clash, argue or fight.*

CONFORM *fitting in with or adapting to the accepted rules or standards. To alter your behaviour to suit others, such as a school or other organization.*

CRITICIZE OR CRITICISM *judging and disapproving of someone or something*

DEFENSIVE *jumping to your own defence when being criticized or attacked*

HYPOCRITICAL *being something you're not or saying something and then behaving in the opposite way*

IMMATURITY *acting younger than is usual for your age*

INSECURITY *lacking confidence or feeling unsure of yourself*

MOTIVATED OR MOTIVATE *wanting to do something or feeling driven to succeed at something*

NEGOTIATING *discussion where you try to reach an agreement or deal that both sides are happy with*

OPTIMISTIC OR OPTIMISM *feeling positive and hopeful. Expecting good things to happen or seeing the best in situations or events.*

PESSIMISTIC OR PESSIMISM *feeling negative and without hope. Expecting the worst to happen or seeing the bad in situations or events.*

PLATONIC *being without desire or romantic feeling. A platonic relationship is usually a friendship between people of the opposite sex who do not have deeper feelings for one another.*

SELF-ESTEEM *respect for yourself. To have self-esteem is to think favourably about the person you are and to be happy about your achievements or the way you behave towards others.*

SENSITIVE *having regard for the feelings of others. To be thoughtful towards other people. To be easily offended or upset.*

SYMPATHETIC OR SYMPATHY *showing understanding towards another person*

THE GET REAL ADVICE DIRECTORY

If you've got a problem and you'd like to talk to a trained professional or counsellor, here are some useful numbers. Don't suffer in silence. These helplines are there to help you and you don't have to give your name.

HELPLINES

ANTI-BULLYING CAMPAIGN 0207 381446
Advice on anything to do with bullying.

CHILDLINE 0800 1111
www.childline.org.uk
For help with any worries or problems.

KIDSCAPE 08451 205204
www.kidscape.org.uk
For help with bullying or abuse.

NSPCC 0808 8005000
www.worriedneed2talk.org.uk
A free counselling and advice line.

THE LINE 0800 2797454
Free counselling for teenagers.

THE SAMARITANS 08457 909090
www.samaritans.org
For help with any worries or problems.

YOUTH 2 YOUTH 0208 8963675
Emotional advice from young people.

OTHER ORGANIZATIONS

AUSTRALIAN DRUG FOUNDATION
www.adf.org.au
The Australian Drug Foundation has a wide range of information on all aspects of drugs, their effects and their legal position in Australia.

CRUSE BEREAVEMENT
www.rd4u.org.co.uk
Confidential advice for those dealing with the death of a close friend or family member.

DRINKWISE
www.drinkwise.co.uk
Advice on anything to do with alcohol.

EATING DISORDERS ASSOCIATION 0845 6347650
www.edauk.com
For those people suffering from an eating disorder, or their friends and family.

FRANK 0800 776600
www.talktofrank.com
For free and confidential advice about drugs and smoking (formerly the National Drugs Helpline).

GET CONNECTED 0808 8084994
www.getconnected.org.uk
For anyone who's run away or been thrown out of their home.

LGBT YOUTHLINE 0845 1130005
Support and advice for young gay people or those confused about their sexuality.

NATIONAL AIDS HELPLINE 0800 567123
For help and advice about AIDS or HIV.

NATIONAL MISSING PERSONS HELPLINE 0500 700700
www.missingpersons.org
Help for the families of missing persons.

RAPE CRISIS 0115 9003560
Support for rape sufferers.

RELATEEN 0845 4561310
For young people wanting to talk about family problems or relationships.